HALF GRAPH
LINED NOTEBOOK

120 Graph – Lined pages, 8,5" x 11"

Additionally: Monthly to do and Password pages

THIS BOOK
BELONGS TO:

_____

MONTHLY TO-DO LIST

JANUARY

- [ ]
- [ ]
- [ ]
- [ ]
- [ ]

FEBRUARY

- [ ]
- [ ]
- [ ]
- [ ]
- [ ]

MARCH

- [ ]
- [ ]
- [ ]
- [ ]
- [ ]

APRIL

- [ ]
- [ ]
- [ ]
- [ ]
- [ ]

MAY

- [ ]
- [ ]
- [ ]
- [ ]
- [ ]

JUNE

- [ ]
- [ ]
- [ ]
- [ ]
- [ ]

JULY

- [ ]
- [ ]
- [ ]
- [ ]
- [ ]

AUGUST

- [ ]
- [ ]
- [ ]
- [ ]
- [ ]

SEPTEMBER

- [ ]
- [ ]
- [ ]
- [ ]
- [ ]

OCTOBER

- [ ]
- [ ]
- [ ]
- [ ]
- [ ]

NOVEMBER

- [ ]
- [ ]
- [ ]
- [ ]
- [ ]

DECEMBER

- [ ]
- [ ]
- [ ]
- [ ]
- [ ]

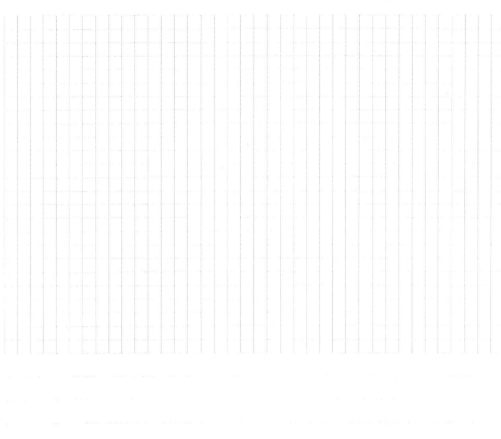

Easy Password Tracker

Site	Username	Password

Easy Password Tracker

Site	Username	Password

Easy Password Tracker

Site	Username	Password

Made in the USA
Monee, IL
30 July 2022